The
Bat-Chen
Diaries

Editor's Notes:

In the original Hebrew, many of Bat-Chen's poems have charming rhymes, which are not reflected in the English translation.

We have chosen to keep the Hebrew words Ima *(mommy) and* Abba *(daddy).*

Many of the entries have been excerpted.

Translated by Diana Rubanenko
Edited by Judyth Groner

Text and art copyright © 2008 The Shahak Family
Photo credits: © Sa'ar Ya'acov/The State of Israel, p. 7; © Ohayon Avi/The State of Israel, p. 35 ; all other photos courtesy of The Shahak Family

Kar-Ben Publishing
A division of Lerner Publishing Group, Inc.
241 First Avenue North
Minneapolis, MN 55401

Website address: www.karben.com

Library of Congress Cataloging-in-Publication Data

Shahak, Bat-Chen.
   The Bat-Chen diaries / by Bat-Chen Shahak.
       p.   cm.
   Includes bibliographical references.
   ISBN-13: 978–0–8225–8807–8 (lib. bdg. : alk. paper
   1. Shahak, Bat-Chen—Juvenile literature. 2. Terrorism--Israel--Juvenile literature. 3. Jewish girls—Israel—Juvenile literature. I. Title.
CT1919.P38.S36722 2008
956.9405'4092—dc22
   [B]   2007005274

Manufactured in the United States of America
1 2 3 4 5 6 – JR – 13 12 11 10 09 08

Table of Contents

Bat-Chen Shahak

In November 1995, Israel's Prime Minister Yizhak Rabin
was gunned down at a peace rally in Tel Aviv. Among the
hundreds of condolence letters received by his widow
Leah, was a poem from a 14-year old teenager, Bat-Chen
Shahak. She wrote eloquently of Rabin's achievements as
a leader and condemned the hatred that led to his death.
What Bat-Chen could not know was that only four
months later she would meet the same fate. In March
1996, Bat-Chen was killed by a suicide bomber in
Tel Aviv's Dizengoff Center. It was Purim. And it was her
15th birthday.

Bat-Chen was named for a flower whose white, pink, and
red blossoms dot the Israeli countryside. From an early
age she loved to write, and in 5th grade she began to
keep a diary where she recorded her feelings and
commented on events around her.

After her death, her family gathered the diaries, along
with notebooks, letters, and drawings. Bat-Chen wrote
birthday greetings to her parents and siblings – Ye'ela and
Ofri; loving eulogies for her grandparents and great-
grandparents; a thank-you letter to her ear doctor. In her
diaries she wrote of school, teachers, and homework; the
angst of young love, the trials of friendship, and dreams
for the future. Bat-Chen loved Jerusalem and wrote of its
beauty and holiness. Her heartfelt poems show her
fervent desire for peace.

Portions of her writings have been published in Hebrew,
and have been translated into Arabic, Japanese, Italian,
Dutch, and German. This is the first English anthology of
her work.

4

"Who has the right to take the most
beautiful gift of all – life?"

Bat-Chen Shahak

To Leah Rabin

Three shots and it's over.
Now one talks about him in the past tense.
Suddenly, the present becomes the past,
And the past is only a memory.

We are standing, crying,
Wanting to believe it never happened.
That it is all a bad dream,
That we'll wake up tomorrow and everything will be ok.

Instead, we wake up to a sad reality,
Where pain is laced with hatred.
We cannot digest the enormity of this loss,
Or comprehend its harshness.

How can we understand such a tragedy?
We don't live in a jungle, but in a civilized country.
Each one of us has a right to his opinion.
It's human nature for people to disagree.

We cannot turn the clock back,
But we can stop for today and remember.
In a few days everything will return to normal for us.
But the family will be left to cope with this abomination!
It's like a domino that falls and causes a chain reaction.
In every sense of the word, we were beheaded,
And now it all crumbles.
It's as if he were the head, and we the body,
And when the head isn't functioning, the body dies!

It's impossible to build a tower with mismatched bricks,
With parts that do not fit.
You need to be a skilled person to build a sturdy tower,
But a single kick can shatter it all — destroy a state,
That was built brick by brick from diverse elements.

I don't understand.
Everyone is rushing to find the guilty parties.
I think we are all guilty,
For not showing how much we loved him.

It's like the mother who tries to educate her children.
And they don't understand what their parents want.
Until they grow up and become parents themselves.
Now after he's dead, suddenly everyone wakes up,
They realize they've suffered a loss.
It's time to repay their debt, so they come,
They write, they cry, they ask for forgiveness.

Maybe I'm too naïve, but I cannot understand
How people can take the law into their own hands!
If someone disagrees with me, do I get up and shoot
   him?
Who has the right to take the most beautiful gift of all –
   of life?
Suddenly we have become one,
Sharing the same fate.
Old and young, we stand embracing one another,
And we cry.

As many have said — even the best writers and poets —
It's impossible to describe you.
Even life itself is overshadowed by your greatness.

I join in the grief of your family and hope that you will
   not know any more sorrow.

Yours,
Bat-Chen

Early
Writing

What I Want From the New Year

No more wars,
For peace to come.
For Maya to be my teacher.
I want to have lots of friends,
And I want us to finish building the new house.

Bat Chen and Tuli

I have a cat who is called Tuli. Tuli was born in Rishpon in the courtyard of my grandmother's apartment and grandma brought him to me in Tel-Mond. It was hard for her to catch him. She brought him to Tel-Mond in a sack. Then he escaped to the neighbors. Afterward in the evening, Ima called me to bring him food, and since then Tuli came into the house every day. One day Tuli disappeared. We thought Tuli had died, but a day passed, then two days. And on the third day Tuli returned.

Bat-Chen: You wrote an interesting story. It was a pleasure to read it—Maya

10

וְנָשִׁיר בְּ כֹל לֵב?

אִם כָּל יוֹם עוֹבֵר וְנֶאֱמָר

בְּ יוֹם לָכֶם שִׁירוֹ לִי הֶפֶר

הַדְּ־חֵן
כְּכַבַּת סְפוֹר
מַלְאָנִין,
הָיָה לְקָמָב
לְבָן וּ
אֵיפֹה בֵּן

To God

I have a few wishes I want to ask.
My first wish is for grandfather to come back to life.
The second is that there won't be any more wars,
The third is that we'll live in peace with all the countries.

Second Grade Exercise Book

What Do You Wish For Your Country?

It's a beautiful, good country that has everything.
It has flowers and trees and butterflies...lots of them.
You can find almost everything you want in this country.
But one thing is missing, and that's peace.
I really miss it.

Every day when I get up and hear on the radio about the
intifada and what's happening, I feel bad and ask Ima:
when will peace come? I'm waiting for it every day, and
call out loud: come on, peace, come already. I call and
call but it hasn't come. I asked Ima why peace doesn't
come but she didn't answer and just stroked my head.

Third Grade Exercise Book

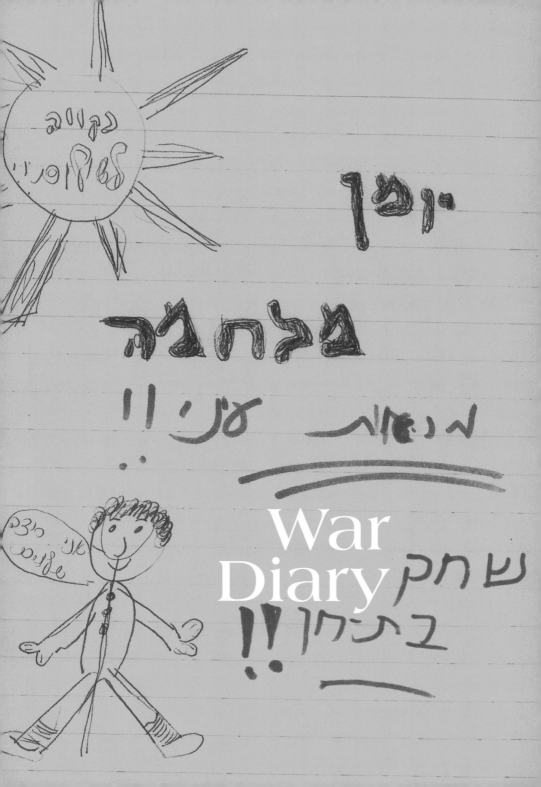

The Gas Mask

No one predicted the war.
Then it came — the siren like a loud roar.
And into the sealed room we ran.
Since this was the first time for this task,
I had an argument with the gas mask.
I said:
"Not only do you make me sick,
And press on my throat,
But you won't let me sleep.
What are you thinking, you insolent thing?"

The gas mask kept quiet,
But suddenly let out a sigh:
"You hurt me!"
And started to cry,
"You should know that I'm only protecting you,
Keeping you from harm."

"Sorry, sorry," I said.
But it still presses on me and makes me nauseous.

"In my opinion," the mask said,
"You'll get used to the situation.
And remember that as long as I'm covering your head,
It's for your own good."

"I have an idea. Why don't we play checkers?"
"Gladly," the mask said.
The two of us then sat and played, forgetting the mask.

So went my first day with the mask.
In the beginning I had a bit of a problem.
But then I got used to it.
I even played with it — and won!

שם: בת חן

מקצוע: היומן של

כתה: הות

ביה"ס: הגאווה

תל אביב

5th Grade
Diary

The Quiz

I got up this morning with a fever, and I only went to school because of the quiz. I was even ready to give up a scouting trip. And when I finished taking it, I realized I didn't pass. I was very angry. How could it happen? A few days later I understood.

Conclusion: You have to learn to lose gracefully. If you don't pass a test, it's not so bad. You must always look at the glass as half full.

Elections

Every year in our school there are elections for all sorts of committees, and this year I wanted to be on the newspaper committee, where you put together newspapers, illustrate them, write features, and edit them. But I was sick that day and wasn't in class, and they held the elections, and someone got one more vote than I did. Perhaps, if I'd been in class, all of us might have been elected. In the end I was elected to another committee.

What can you do? Whenever something important happens, suddenly I start sneezing! "Take it easy, that's life!" That's the conclusion I drew from this event.

Me

Dear diary, I haven't introduced myself.
OK, so my name's Bat-Chen and I'm in class 5/a.

I decided to write a diary
And tell everything that happens in my life —
When I'm happy and also when I'm sad.
And I decided that keeping a diary
Will be a beautiful memento of my childhood.
Even when I'm down — when I'm nervous and angry,
The diary changes my life into something more beautiful.

And in the diary I'll tell about my friend Chen,
And the two Nildassys* who get on my nerves,
And make life dark and gloomy,
But I try to overcome this.
And I'll write about things that happen each day.

** Bat Chen gave the name
"Nildassys" to her two
friends Nili and Hadas*

What An Irritating Mother!

I was playing with the computer today,
And suddenly it froze.
I went downstairs
And my little sister ran after me
And said to Ima, "Bat-Chen cursed at me!"

Then, without thinking,
Ima started scolding me,
"What an awful child!"

And of course it wasn't true.
You can imagine how angry and insulted I was.

I had a tangerine in my hand and threw it straight at Ima.
It messed up the tablecloth a bit,
And you can guess what happened:

She yelled at me and sent me to my room.
When I wanted a drink,
She stood on the staircase and said,
"Say you're sorry at once!"
So I said to her:
"What are you — a queen or something?"
Then she said, "Don't you dare leave your room."
I went back to my room and hung a sign on the door:
"No entry to idiots!"
Wouldn't you be irritated too
If people made up things about you?
And Ima's sure that she's right, that she's so smart.
And she's furious with me.

Chen

Apart from the irritating Nildassys,
There's also Chen, a clever, quiet and sweet girl.
She's my best friend.
And how can you measure a good friend?
You measure them in times of trouble,
And I'll you give an example:
When I didn't pass the test, Chen said:
"Never mind. Look, you reached the third level,
And that's still a high one."
I love her very much.
She's always ready to help, and she loves life —
To laugh, to sing, and to have fun.
I like doing projects with her,
Chatting and talking and being around her.
I wish there were more kids like her.

She doesn't have to be the best,
Like that lovely couple, the Nildassys.
What's important to Chen is being a best friend,
And I really appreciate her.

To Chen, Thanks for your help and support
You really are a good friend.

Ye'ela

I swear to you, that girl is a real pain.
Always pestering me and tattling on me.
She's a very bad girl.
And Ima isn't very nice.
She thinks Ye'ela is the queen.

Luckily there's an Abba in the world!
Because Ima and Ye'ela really drive me crazy,
Especially Ye'ela who thinks she deserves everything!
Dear diary, I'm furious,
My little sister gets on my nerves.

Ye'ela,
When you want to be, you're a wonderful sister.
It's a shame that this diary
Will have some not so wonderful things in it.
That's what I've decided.

$O$of - Another Operation

I've had ear problems since I was a year old. Now I'm eleven, and I've already had four operations, and lots of ear-cleaning sessions, check-ups, and so on. Next Monday I'm going to have a fifth operation. I don't want that day to come. Even though I've gotten used to it already, I'm still afraid, and all sorts of thoughts float into my head:

What if I never wake up?
Perhaps I'll be brain-damaged!
Or even deaf, heaven forbid!

It's very hard to explain. You have to undergo an operation to know what fear really is. Before the fourth operation, the nurse said to me: "You know, Bat-Chen, it's natural, everyone's scared. And if someone says he isn't, it's a sign he's lying."

It's just the uncertainty about what's going to happen afterwards that's so frightening — and also the anesthetics. I don't want the operation, but there's no alternative, I've got to have it!

Dear diary, you'll be with me during the operation, won't you?

이니

7th Grade Diary

A Poem Marking the End of Elementary School

It's the final moment. Waving our report cards in farewell,
Standing and crying, lost for words.
We had good times within these four walls.
It wasn't only the grades and the classes.
It was much more, and we don't want to give it up.

Though it's over and done, everyone wants to go back.
Some kids bring out their albums,
And everyone recalls the days when we were little.
Hang on, don't go.
Let's take one more photo before the big farewell.
We'll never be the same again —
A class that helped in every way.
That's it, it's over.

I don't know what to call you — diary, notebook? I'll be writing down everything you feel when you start Junior High. So the best name is "Transition to Junior High."

Yesterday I got the note telling me which class I'm going to be in. It wasn't really news as I already knew the teacher's name — Idit. And I'm going to be in class Z/9, with the kids from Ma'ayan Vered and two other girls from Tel-Mond. But what difference does it really make?

We got an invitation to Team-Building Day, and I'm already wondering about the teacher. Perhaps she'll be a cruel witch with a long nose, riding on a broomstick. Or maybe she'll be a beautiful blonde and very nice.

And what will the other kids be like? Nice? Fun to be with? Or maybe my class will be gross! Well, I'm terribly excited. Okay I'll update you after the Team-Building Day. Talk to you later, my "Transition to Junior High."

With Love

P.S. Without insulting you, it's a bit weird to be writing "with love." You're just a book with lines. Don't be offended, it just seems weird.

We've Begun

We arrived. The new beginning was awaiting us there in the corner. We've already written the date, the subject, and the teacher's name in a notebook. I wondered all summer what the beginning would be like — if a good fairy leads us into a tunnel, and once you're out, you can say, "I've done the beginning. It was easy. All I had to do was enter the tunnel." But when I walked into the classroom, the teacher was waiting. Nothing like a good fairy.

What does a beginning look like? Is it hard or easy?
A beginning is when something ends and begins anew,
Like a flower that droops, then blooms once more.

"Beginnings, beginnings."
I heard the word hundreds of times in 6th grade!
And in many other places.

So we began our beginning.
We tasted a slice of the cake.
At the beginning it will be sweet:
Meeting new people and also new subjects.
But later it'll get awful and we'll want it to end,
To start the next year – a new beginning.

The Transition to Junior High

I'm sorry I haven't written much. I've had a lot of problems in class, and came home in tears quite often. I had no idea the beginning would be so difficult....a bit like a baby who can't walk at first, and it starts and then suddenly topples over. That's exactly what I feel like. Everyone has a tough start - the teacher, that baby trying to walk ... but it'll be ok in the end.

Yom *Kippur*

Dear Diary,
Today is Yom Kippur,
And I have been fasting for 21 hours.
It's very hard. Every moment I feel like giving in.
I count the seconds, and try to pass time,
But it's hard because my stomach hurts.
I take comfort in the fact that most of it is behind me,
And soon I'll be able to eat.
Do you have an idea for something to keep me busy?
Because that's what I need.
My stomach hurts and it's waiting to be filled with food.

My Great-Grandmother

Dear Diary:

Generally everything's ok in class and it's only when
something unusual happens that I feel I must write to
you. Something very sad happened which I want to
share. I'm privileged to have something that most children
don't have — a great-grandmother. When I was eight,
whenever we visited Grandma Naomi, I'd run to see my
great-grandmother Rivka. I don't remember that much
because her condition started to deteriorate and she
became very old and hardly remembered me! But it is
because of her that I love garlic. She would always serve
me tomato with garlic, and egg with garlic. I really loved
visiting her and loved her as a person. In her later years,
old age destroyed her, and whenever I saw her, it broke
my heart.

Now she's had a stroke, and today I went to visit her in
the hospital. She's unconscious and half of her body is
paralyzed. I burst into tears and there was no stopping
them. I know in my heart it's the end — there's a smell
of death in the air. I feel that very soon the time will
come, and they'll take her in a chariot to the next world.
She deserves to be in heaven because life wasn't kind to
her. Two of her children died, and her husband too. It's
hard for me to see her like this, helpless and not reacting.

I'm not fooling myself that she'll live, but I'm trying to be
optimistic. I'm looking at the world — at the trees, the
clouds, everything God made. Maybe if Adam and Eve
had been a little nicer, we wouldn't know what death and
suffering mean. Great-grandma is suspended between
heaven and earth now, and it's only God's grace that will
decide her fate. She is a good woman and I am happy
that I had the opportunity to know her – at least a little.

What is death? For me it remains a puzzle. People die just like children are born. It's part of nature. One day a baby is born, bringing joy to the family. Everyone smiles and is happy. And on the same day another human being dies and another family is in terrible mourning. But they have to get back to routine. It's difficult, and the closer you are the harder it is. Saying goodbye is always difficult.

I'm a girl who just can't understand why people die. I cry at night; it hurts me. God, please tell me why.
Why does it have to happen?
Why do we have to grow old?
Why can't we always stay young?
Why can't life be perfect like in fairytales?
Why, oh why? — the words pose a question.
Who's going to give me an answer?
Only one's imagination can provide answers.

He Passes Me By

Every day another person's life ends.
But He passes me by.
I hope that He won't also take me.
It's unknown. It's unforseen.

You can come back from school and find
You have no father, or grandpa,
Or brother or sister, or uncle or aunt.

And you say:
Only yesterday he stood beside me,
Only yesterday he hugged me.
Only yesterday he was laughing,
Only yesterday he kissed my cheek.
Only yesterday he wrapped me in warmth and love.
Only yesterday he encouraged me.

It's interesting that death occupies my thoughts.
Many times I keep thinking and I repeat:
Only yesterday, only yesterday...

There are no goodbyes with death.
He decides that today it's your turn,
And He will take you.
And He will care for your family from above.
You don't suffer anymore, or feel anymore.
But the people who remain behind suffer, disbelieving.

Only yesterday we sang and laughed,
And maybe even quarreled.
It can happen any day.
Oh dear, so many troubles!

Dear Diary: I'm not going to write anything about school. Everything is irritating and annoying, so I'd rather write about my thoughts and feelings.

Love

Love is a word that isn't in the dictionary.
Everyone defines it differently.
For me there are two kinds of love:
Love for father and mother, brother and sister,
For a best friend and for the family in general.
This kind of love is different from love for a boy.

For me the foundation of love is honesty,
Because without honesty you can't build a relationship.
Love means giving a part of yourself to your loved one,
And keeping the other part for yourself.

Love is a wonderful thing, but it's like a game.
You have to follow the rules, otherwise it's a broken heart,
And a broken heart is an aching heart, missing a piece.
A piece that makes the heart whole.

The heart determines love.
It's not that I suddenly decide that I love him.
The heart tells me what to do, gives me orders.
The heart is like parents, setting the rules.
The heart chooses for me,
And since it's my heart, I accept its choice
And trust its discretion.

Love is built on mutual trust.
Love is giving and receiving.
Love is something shared: half of me and half of you.
And together we'll create a special heart,
One of a kind.

Songs

For me, writing is something wonderful.
It makes me a happy person.
Songs are everything to me.

Whenever I feel down, and things are hard,
I sit myself down and begin to write —
About the past and about the present,
About the future.

I write down feelings.
And what I love doing best is imagining
How people resemble plants,
And how friendship between people
Is like a flower and water.

Whenever I feel down, and things are hard,
I pick up my notebook and pen and write.
With songs I feel lighter, more distant.
I feel like it's just me and the song,
Saying what we think about the world.
And no one says, "This is forbidden, this is permitted."
A song has no framework, no rules.

We can sing whatever we want.
It takes you away from sadness,
Even though you know
That a song lasts only a few moments.

A song is not just a tune for me,
It's not just words that you sing,
And when it's over that's it.
For me, it's life itself. It's a special world.

And you don't have to be in my shoes
To understand that writing means forgetting everything
And entering into an imaginary world,
A world that's mine alone,
A world that sees things differently,
And opens up a loving heart.
In that world, you don't have to account to anyone else.

This is my world, and nobody will take it from me.
God gave it to me.
He gives a gift to each one of us,
And to me He gave me my little world.
Otherwise I don't know how I'd manage.
Because the real world,
The one that's yours and mine and everyone's,
Is a difficult world with so many problems,
And with so much frustration.

I open the diary and remember
Everything I've written in that world,
A world that is just mine and yours.
A tranquil world, a world of rest.

Ron Arad

Suddenly, I find myself sitting and writing. I don't even know him or his family personally. He's become famous — in Israel and in a large part of the world.

Famous: when someone is famous it's usually because he did something that attracted the attention of the media — an act of heroism; or because he is a government minister, an actor or entertainer, a beauty queen. There are other things that make people famous, some of them are good deeds, some of them are bad ones.

Let's get back to Ron.
Almost every child knows his name now.
Ron Arad is a prisoner, sitting in a dark place,
Where iron bars are the only thing he sees.
And how do they explain it to little Yuval?
"Daddy can't come home; he's a prisoner."

Whenever there's a TV program about him,
Everybody watches and weeps.
Everyone feels terribly angry.
How can they do it?
He's got a family and friends.
Why does he have to live in prison for so many years?
After all, what did he do?
He served his country faithfully like any citizen.

Then once the program ends, people switch off the TV and get on with their lives. They've already forgotten what they saw on television yesterday. Only Tammy, with her photo album and a few memories, is left knowing that at that very minute he could be with her. She thinks they could be enjoying themselves.

He doesn't even know his little girl.
Tammy wonders: Has he seen the sun recently?
Does he hear the birds singing?
The words "freedom" and "liberty"
Are just a dream for him,
But should not remain a dream.

What has he been doing there all these years?
Does he just sit and look at the iron bars?
How do they treat him?
It's time that people understand that
Ron Arad is more than a headline.
Behind the headlines are so much pain and frustration,
And the yearnings of a man who did not have good luck.

Tammy has done almost everything possible.
When she wakes up in the morning, during the day,
And in the evening all she thinks about is Ron.
Where does her hope and faith come from?
Where does she get the strength to stand so tall?
Where does she get her trust that he'll return.
To the bosom of his family?
It's simply awful!

Ron Arad is an Israeli Air Force navigator who has been missing in action since 1986. Yuval is his daughter, Tammy is his wife.

The Funeral

What I feared has happened: my dear great-grandmother
has died. There were lots of phone-calls that day and
Grandma Naomi said: "There's nothing to be done. It's
very painful but life must go on."

But the funeral was very difficult for her. She wept out
loud and I'll never forget Ofri's big eyes, looking for
answers, trying to solve the puzzle. Why is that person
standing there crying? He doesn't understand the meaning
of the word "died." He doesn't understand what it means
that Grandma is no longer alive.

And Grandma Naomi tries to explain.
It's hard when someone who raised you, has died.
She laughed and cried, danced and sang –
And now there's nothing left of her,
Nothing left to remind us.
Only a big stone, declaring to passers-by that
Under the stone is a woman — like you and me —
Just a stone, unresponsive,
Standing there saying Great-Grandma has died.

The funeral was tough.
Grandma laid a wreath of flowers and said,
"She was a noble woman," and choked back her tears.

*J*ews and Arabs 37

For some of us the word "Arab" brings to mind a knife in the back, death, rocks, murders, molotov cocktails, burning tires, terrorists, the Hezbollah.

Some of us make a distinction: There are Arab murderers just as there are Jewish ones. Every country has its good and bad people. And there are some who will say, "The Arabs are our best friends; they too have the right to live."

There is a lot of unrest in our little country. There are three opinions on Arabs: the settlers and the Radical Right reject the Arabs; the Left makes a distinction, and the Radical Left demands rights for the Arabs too!

It's very hard for me to make up my mind about which position to take. One moment I'm for the Left, then suddenly the radio announcer says, "Jews have been murdered, the terrorists have been captured," and I say: "It could have been one of my family!"

All this hatred began more than 2,000 years ago. And we and the Arabs have not been able to resolve it. I always say there are good Arabs too. But in the meantime, I only hear about the murderers.

I want peace and believe in the end there will be peace.
Because it is vital for the continuation of life.
The question is what kind of peace?
Peace like the one with the Palestinians is not peace.
On both sides the people are angry.
Peace is a beautiful word with a wonderful meaning.
A word of value and significance.
Every day and every hour,
We talk of peace — directly or indirectly.

The Holocaust

Ima, tell me what happened 50 years ago.
What does that horrible word mean — "Holocaust?"
Ima, please tell me.

Come, child, I'll tell you what happened
To our people in the countries of the diaspora.
Come, come child.
Once there were many flowers in my garden,
Big beautiful flowers.
I let them grow and flourish, left them in peace.
My flowers were more beautiful than any others.

I had an irritating neighbour whose flowers didn't grow.
Out of jealousy (I was probably sleeping at the time),
As a sign of revenge,
He decided to cut down all the flowers in the garden,
Leaving only bare earth.
Some of them survived because they had to go on living
To insure there would be future generations.

Ima, where are the flowers now?

Almost all the flowers have withered.
And those that managed to survive also lost some petals.

What a nasty neighbour!
Why did he do it? the girl asked.
So was that the Holocaust, Ima?
The flowers that withered in your lovely garden?

Oh, no, child.
The lovely, blossoming flowers.
They were our people, the Jews,
The evil neighbor was Hitler and the Germans.

But why? What for?
The girl asked, not understanding.

One day you wake up and they've disappeared,
Slipped through your fingers.
And you ask where have the lovely flowers gone?
All you have left is the bare earth,
Earth that causes you pain whenever you tread on it.
The whole story repeats itself.
You hear your brothers' blood cry out from the earth,
The despair and suffering they went through —
Those who survived despite all the torture.

They had one goal —
To reach their homeland and to tell their story,
So that everyone will remember
The beautiful flowers that once lived
And one day suddenly vanished.

Ima, why did they suffer? Why were they killed?
Because they were Jews and not Germans?
Starved and tortured in labor camps,
In the awful gas chambers?
Why aren't they still alive?

Dear child, I, too, will never know the answers.
Tears pour from my eyes.
I want you to know that those who remained
Will never again be the loveliest flowers in the garden.
They have scars for the rest of their lives,
Scars that will never fade.
At night the terrible scenes return.
Many won't be able to visit my garden,
And those who do will be in a terrible mood
After they see the destruction.

Child, sweet child,
That was their first hell:
Blows, killing, humiliation, hunger,
Labor camps, gas chambers.
In a word — the Holocaust.

From the Holocaust we learn
That we can no longer live among foreigners.
We will live only where we have rights —
In the Jewish homeland!

This was just some of what happened to the Jews
Over the years and throughout that period.
And I can say without question
That it was the worst thing.

"Remember! And never forget what the
Nazi Amalek did to you." I'll always keep that
declaration in my heart.

Life is Starting to be Boring

Hello, Dear Diary!
Life is starting to be boring and I'm trying to fight it.
Every morning the same thing,
Repeating itself, like a broken record.

Getting up each morning, doing the usual things —
Getting dressed, combing my hair, like all the kids.
No amazing experiences, no daring adventures,
Nothing exciting to make me jump out of bed at 6:30.
Instead I could keep sleeping sweetly.
And at school it's even worse —
Tests and more tests, to see who's the best.
And the teacher gives assignments:
"Just four or five pages, it's so little, what's the problem?"
And we're all stressed.
Today a test, another tomorrow. Oof! It never ends.
So it's back home again,
Doing homework and studying for tests.

To put it simply, I don't like this kind of life.
Everything is so ordered and fixed.
Everything goes in a straight line without a single turn.

No parties on Fridays.
And if there are, they aren't special.
OK, so the girls get together to gossip,
But after such a boring day, there's not much to say.
I really long for a sudden surprise —
Something special, outstanding, unique,
Something just for me will suddenly happen.

Perhaps an English prince has chosen me for his bride,
And from now I'll live in a palace,
Where everyone bows down to me.
I'll be famous and all the newspapers will write about me.
But at some point even being a princess
And living in a palace will get boring.

So, perhaps I'll win a trip abroad — to a far-off jungle,
Where life doesn't happen according to the rules.
Watching the people there could be really interesting —
Traveling through the wild, seeing monkeys and elephants.
And if I really get lucky,
Perhaps I'll see Tarzan, King of the Apes,
Swinging through the branches.

I think that you should be able to try everything,
To taste a bit of this and that,
To travel the world and meet all kinds of people.
Life ought to be more spontaneous, flexible,
Not a life you simply exist in,
Rigid and fixed, void of experience,

I really want to be different, not like everyone else.
To do something different,
That makes me stand out from the crowd,
To be someone whom everyone stares at.
Anything — just not to lead such a regular life,
Without content or meaning,
This kind of life must be a mistake!

Nobody's Perfect!

Nobody's perfect, and that's the way of the world.
Perhaps the Creator planned it that way ages ago,

We're all different from each other, like it or not.
Actually, if you think about it,
What a boring life we'd have if we were all the same.

God gave each of us one thing
That makes us stand out from others:
One person is smart, and — what can you do? —
Another is an idiot.
Some are good-looking, and others are ugly.
You could go on until tomorrow listing every trait.

But when you add it all up, we're all pretty much alike,
Some are exceptional — for example retarded people.
But it's not their fault.
And every human who is a little different,
Is seen by society as strange.
Society doesn't know how to accept someone different,
Someone with a flaw.

Instead of accepting, society condemns.
Instead of offering help,
Instead of understanding the misfortune,
Society causes harm.
So who wants to live in a hurtful society?
After all, nobody's perfect.
Each of us has some flaw.
Perhaps it's not an obvious one, but it's there inside you.
So why is it society's nature to be so cruel?

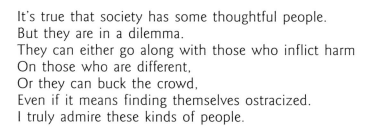
It's true that society has some thoughtful people.
But they are in a dilemma.
They can either go along with those who inflict harm
On those who are different,
Or they can buck the crowd,
Even if it means finding themselves ostracized.
I truly admire these kinds of people.

Has society ever considered
How hurtful this is to the person who is different?
He has to learn how to cope with his plight!
It's not his fault, so why can't we accept him?

What I Want To Be When I Grow Up

Lots of kids worry about this question:
What will they do when they're grown up?
Everyone thinks about the future.
It's always following us, like a kind of shadow.
No one can tell exactly what's going to happen.
But we all try to predict it.

One wants to be a doctor, because it's the way she sees
That she will be able to help others and save lives.
One wants to be a policeman,
Because to him a policeman seems to be the image
Of a good, educated person,
Who sets a good example for his country.
He believes it is to his credit
That our citizens will all be law-abiding.

One wants to be an artist
And to paint each town and village.
And his work, he believes,
Will show people how life really is
From different perspectives.
They may even want to get inside the picture
And stay there for ever.
That's what he thinks will make people happy.

One wants to be a teacher, so that in the future
She can make the changes she thinks are really needed.
So there will be good, concerned teachers,
Certainly different from those who teach us now.
She wants to change everything, and why not?
If she can change the rules and make learning wonderful?

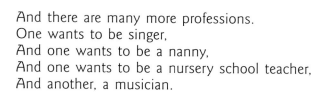

And there are many more professions.
One wants to be singer,
And one wants to be a nanny,
And one wants to be a nursery school teacher,
And another, a musician.

Professions range from teacher to policeman,
But all of them have one thing in common.
All of them, in one way or another,
Want to help people and the country
Live better and brighter lives.

And they believe that they can build,
Make changes where they're needed,
And preserve what is desirable.
And of course, they themselves want to enjoy life
And give joy to others as much as they can!
So we all hope that their wishes come true.

And what do I want to be?
You must have guessed!
Right! I want to convey my feelings and thoughts
Through melodies and words that join together.
To create songs, songs that will lighten people's lives,
And make them look at problems from new perspectives.

The Vanishing Notebook

Hello, dear diary:
I want to tell you a story
That started badly and ended well.

Last Saturday night I wanted to study for a Bible test.
(I really love Bible.)
I got to my room and the notebook was not on the desk.
Not in the drawer,
Not under the bed,
Not in the piles of clothes,
And not in my parents' room.
Notebook notebook, where are you hiding?
Come out of there, I've no time for games.
Come on, notebook, stop making me crazy.

I organized a search party —
To do everything necessary to find the notebook.
I tried my best to think back but it didn't help.
I became totally hysterical, losing control,
And all because of a pile of pages, stapled together.

The chances of finding it were slim, and
I was on the brink of desperation.
In such a big house anything can get lost.
I felt awful, but luckily my grandmother was around.
She's a special grandma, and I'm not just saying that.
She knows how to get out of difficult situations.

And as the tears flowed,
She began to put on a comedy act for me.
In the end, there was no option but to go to sleep
Without my friend (the notebook).

Next morning, we got in the car, and there it was!
Oh God, thank you, thank you!
Who would have dreamed it would be in the car?
What a discovery!

And Granny smiled at me:
"Was it worth crying about? What kind of girl are you?"
"I'm a sweetheart," I told her happily.
And Granny said: "Sweetheart, hah!"

Disappointed Love

Disappointed love is so painful —
When you love someone,
But know that his heart belongs to someone else,
That he's not really interested in you,
And you're wasting your time.

His girlfriend is my biggest enemy.
It's all because of her.
If she didn't exist, I could capture him!
Oh, I can see how everything would be perfect,
If only - if only she wasn't around!
Oof! The heck with her!

And the worst is seeing them kissing.
If only I could exchange places with her,
How great it would be!

Why did he choose her?
Is she more beautiful or smart?
Or maybe it's just because he met her first.

Lots of people know about diaries.
Others think a diary is something weird.
So, I just want you to know that my diary is a real help,
With all the problems I have to overcome.

My diary is my best friend.
It never gossips about me,
And never badmouths me.
It never argues, and never disappoints.

It doesn't interrupt when I'm talking,
Or say irritating things.
It never preaches to me,
Or criticizes me, or hurts me.

Nothing can replace it,
There's nothing better.
It listens and lets me pour out my heart,
Without having to boast.

I feel free to tell it everything,
Without worrying that it will reveal anything,
Or let something slip out.
I know it's a real friend.

Its silence symbolizes understanding and concern.
It's warm and loving, never moody.
And it's always open.

We can have fun together,
It encourages me in difficult moments.
And it does all this without words.
Simply awesome!

School's Out (Dedicated to Class 7D)

School's out. Everyone's very happy.
But the end of classes affects our social life.
It'll be a little hard getting up tomorrow,
Not being able to see everyone,
And having to find ways to pass the time.
Suddenly everything's changed!
So I want to record the whole year for posterity.
To recall everything from our first meeting:

Worried looks,
A little shyness,
Lots of hopes,
Hearts pounding.

Everything looks so huge, so complicated.
The teachers seem tough, and there are lots of new faces.
Right away there is a schedule of tests,
And so many pieces of paper.
New requirements for "absences and late arrivals."
For the first time you learn the words "cutting classes."
There's a new subject — Agriculture,
Boring — it must be a mistake.

Now the guys are more interesting,
And you don't notice how you're changing!
From scared, shy children, we've turned into kids
Who couldn't give a (rude word) about the teachers.
In class, you look for original ways to pass notes,
Without attracting the teacher's attention.
You eat in class, and drink as well.
In other words, you have a great time.
But still, there's no choice — we have to study!

There's constant conflict with the teachers.
Everyone wants to irritate them, and be one of the guys.

There was the counselor who taught us sex-education —
We understood more than she did!

And Motti:
When he turns up, everyone quiets down.
All it takes is one look, and fear strikes us all.
The word goes out: "Motti's coming!
Sit down if you don't want to catch it!"

And when we all cram into Freddy's kiosk,
The chances of buying something are slim.
Ada, the teacher, so nice and understanding!
Wish I could say that about Bruria, the witch with horns,
Who grabs us by the ears.

Sarit, who is constantly showing off, is leaving us.
And Fat Seffy who is carrying twins in her stomach.
And Yarden who thinks she's the most considerate.
And Ahuva: "Stop talking!"
Even if you're not talking at all, she's always saying that.
Right, Ahuva?

Miri, who analyzes ballads until you could die,
And everyone is falling asleep.
And sweet Orit, fascinating and clever.
What a fantastic teacher!

If I haven't mentioned other teachers,
It's because they're total zeroes,
Not great and not terrible,
So they don't have the honor of being mentioned here!

That's it, that's how the year went!
Some days were boring, others full of gossip!
It's not so easy saying goodbye.
Next year, the whole thing, like a wheel,
Will start again: teachers, kids — until you adjust.
That was our class. I'll always remember it.

It's a period that's ending.
And a new start awaits us next year.
Who knows what it'll bring?
Eyes full of hope again,
Let it be a great year!

Now the report card seems so unimportant,
So very dull!
Just grades that don't reflect what you've learned.
And it's possible that the computer could be wrong!
It's just a report card.
I don't need it to tell me if I'm good and smart.
Because inwardly I know what I'm worth.

I've written everything I remember!
My hand is tired and I need some rest!
I'm trying not to fear the future!
So bye for now!

אהבה!

אהבה זה כבר הכול, לתת את כל אשר רק
אפשר לתת ולקבל בחזרה. ♥
באהבה יש תקווה, באהבה בגיל ? שמקנים
ובגיל לאלץ להתקרב אל הכפור
ובהרבה שמשמר באהבה את כל התווי איך מתי
לכל אחד יש דרך לבטא אהבה, כי כל אחד
רואה בזאת הבנה שונה.
אהבה זה אני ואתה, שעוד בידק מרגישים אותה
באהבה בגיל לבטות רבים ברשתינו של הפנים
לחבק, לשמוח, לשמור. להרגיש להתאהב מהתחלה
להתגעגע אל ההתחלה.
יש אהבה שהיא גם אהבת תמרים הולכים
ממש כאו עיניים. ♥
באהבה נקנים קונים, כי איא לא מניים
אל פעם בני יהודים, ונזכרים את
סוד אהבה, שמרים הרבה אהבה, ולשמרם
מה לעלות היה את מנה
באהבה יש שני דפפים הבא והרע
כיום הם תמיד צצות, והם אל

Love is Mutual

Love is mutual.
Giving everything you have to the one you love,
And getting it back.

With love there are rules,
And two players who have to play by the rules.

The moment love arrives, it fills your whole life.
Love is me and you, together making a whole.
In love, you have to learn about the other,
To ignore shortcomings, and look at the advantages.
To understand, forgive, and forget.

Love means losing your head, walking ahead blindly.
You take risks in love,
For if you never try you'll never know.
You can taste love: Sometimes it's a delicious cake,
But other times it can be bitter. What can you do?

Love has two sides.
The good and bad are, of course, friends,
And they're never parted, so there's no good without bad,

There's no definition for love in the dictionary.
Each one defines it differently!
Sometimes love is like a notebook,
You finish one and start another.

What is love? It's hard to explain.
It's two pieces.
And finding the missing piece, the one that fits best,
Is the secret of life.
And until you find it, you try everything,
Waiting for the big moment.

58

יומן!

Summer
Diary

TRAUB

789750 .טל ירוש תלפיות | האומן

If You've Opened This

If you've opened this book,
Please respect my privacy and close it.
Because I trust people, I didn't hide or lock it, like most do.
I know this doesn't look like a diary, but it is.
So please don't betray my trust in people,
And respect my wishes.
I know you're curious, but it's not the place or the time.
Some things written here might hurt or infuriate you.
I'll appreciate your overcoming your curiosity
And not opening it!
Poking around isn't a good quality; it can even be harmful.
Thanks so much.
And maybe there will come a day,
When you read this in a newspaper. Who knows?

I Always Wanted To Say It, But I Was Embarrassed!

This year there was a new boy called Omri. I want to explain the situation, and to write the words I've kept in my heart, words which were never let out into the world, until you were created, dear diary.

Love is a wonderful thing. In our class, people haven't paired up yet, except during the couples' dances we do in dance class. That's the reason I didn't dare say a word. Everyone loves someone and if they say it's not so, believe me, they're lying. At first it's just laughs (from embarrassment). But later when they realize what's happening, they become shy. In the end love triumphs and the two people become a couple. These are the words I always wanted to say: That love is never-ending.

Dear diary, I'm happy I can confide in you without anyone revealing my secret. And, at last, after almost a year, I can say the word "love."

60

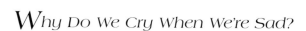

Why Do We Cry When We're Sad?

When we're sad, it's a sign that good things aren't happening. We try to keep things inside, to hold back. And when you can't any longer, then tear drops start to fall quickly, one after the other, just like clouds. Sometimes they're beautiful and white, sometimes dark and gloomy.

We cry for many reasons. There are tears of conflict, when you argue with friends. These teardrops are small, and after a few minutes they dry, and you make up and it's over. End of story.

And sometimes after an operation when you're very, very tense you cry. And the tears are not from pain, but from anxiety and fear of the unknown.

But the most horrible of all is when you lose someone close. Because then you never stop crying, and the tears come slowly and heavily, and they never end. You're crying every day and every hour even if it doesn't show on the outside. Because this is not like a quarrel that can end. This stays with you for life.

To Professor Marshak, My Ear Doctor

Before I came to you, lots of doctors treated me.
But the first time I met you, I knew
That you'd make me happy and carefree,
And that with you it would be different.

Before you touched my ear, you always let me know
That you don't have frightening instruments,
And everything would happen calmly and quietly.

Since I came to you, I've realized that it's not so awful.
You're always ready to help,
And, of course, you do everything
With a sense of humor.

Thanks!

לאחיקם

5.12.90

לבני שאלך באהבה,
על ימי הרבה נוגעת שובתי
שלום אחרי המסע הארוך אל נפשי
שמחתי בזאת שמחה ותקותי
ונוסף בה היה יותרת

לבני שאתה באזן עזר
אהבה לאנא אלוהים ניגע ?
אלל אנל עשירה טסם מאינום
והגיל עשיר בית ♡ והשלוה.

אנא שאנך הסתו, הבנתי על ♡
כן ברא.
ונאהב כן תאהיב מאדן בסור ולאמן
שבכף נעשה בהושע

בהצלחה !

שלם בתוכן

For Chen

When a flower blooms, it is a lovely sight.
We love looking at at it.
Everyone wants to be like a flower —
Beautiful, impressive and admired.
You're like a flower,
You set an example for other flowers.
They're also in the garden but they aren't as beautiful.
Why don't you reveal your secret?

You have six petals, each with a special quality:

1. You're considerate
2. You help others
3. You're concerned and caring
4. You're smart
5. You're charming
6. You're beautiful

Six petals form one whole beautiful flower called Chen.
I've already said that you can measure a good friend in
times of trouble, and you've so often proved that. Our
friendship is like a flower in water. When the flower
droops and suffers, the water revives it, and it straightens
up again. It's the same with us. When I have a problem
or when I'm very sad, to whom do I turn if not Chen,
my best friend. We help each other and we grow and
mature in the big world, take our steps together, and
learn from each other's experiences.

I wish you lots of luck, and may you always be like you
are now. Have a special birthday, because a special girl
deserves a special birthday.

To Grandpa Raffi, Of Blessed Memory

As soon as we started on the road towards Jerusalem, all sorts of thoughts entered my head: What will happen if he doesn't get over that awful illness? It was a terrible feeling, waiting for the unknown, unable to help him. The whole family sang a nursery rhyme to Ofri (who was a year-old then):

> We're going to Yerushalayim,
> Grandma will knit garbayim (socks,)
> Grandpa will buy na'alayim (shoes).

We reached Jerusalem, and there was tension in the air. Everyone was waiting for the moment when we could breathe freely. I remember that Yoav walked in and said, "It's over. We'll never see Grandpa again."

Now I'll tell you how we are coping. I live with the memories forever carved in my mind, of those beautiful days which sadly were so few.

Grandpa, remember when we came to visit you in the hospital. All of your grandchildren peered in through the window, and you waved at us and smiled. That was the last time. Then we said goodbye, like always, but this time it was different. It was a not just parting, it was parting from life — when you say goodbye forever. And you don't meet again except in dreams and in stories, where the life of a great man is hidden between the lines.

You served in the army and won many awards. You were an expert in dominoes and always beat me.

So much has changed since you left us. And I am sure you would be proud of your grandchildren.

Without you everything is different.
It's like a picture fell off the wall, and a piece broke off.
It's impossible to replace it despite how much we try.
Now the picture looks much less beautiful.
Because the missing piece was so necessary.
And nothing we can do will make the picture whole again.
We just have to get used to the missing piece.
Now Grandma has to play two roles.

One thing I'm sure about:
That the piece which fell off wanted us to continue
To be a loving, happy family,
And we have to continue that task,
Even though I don't want to.

To Chen!

We were good friends,
And today we're breaking up.
It's rather hard to use the past tense,
But there's nothing I can do. It's over.

We were together in good times and bad,
And overcame many obstacles.
Now, as I write these lines I'm crying.
I loved you and I always will.
There will always be a corner in my heart
For you and you alone.
You were like a twin sister; we were so perfectly matched!
Something inside is urging me,
"Write it all down! Let all of your feelings out!"

We are ending a long period of very close friendship.
It was hard at the beginning.
Without you I can't go on. Suddenly, I feel empty.
I can't get through the day without saying hello to Chen.

Chen, I loved so much in you,
But even with the good there is bad.
What needs to be said is that it was great.
We should look at the glass that is full.

So today, when you go home,
I want you to remember only the good things —
Like the trips we took together and so many other things.
Today, each of us goes her own way.
And to you, Chen, I wish success.

Each night before you go to sleep,
Devote some of your thoughts to me.

69

לאבא ראמא
היקרים!

אנחנו שמחים שהבאת חברתם!!

חוצרים לעזרה לבוב ולוב
שוב היה הרח הבוב עם הבושל
ושלו אבא ישבו תענג
ושל אבא. תבגה לבוב לבגל

ואבא יעבר בואה על ברהתם מים באבביר
אבנו בהתך!, ואבא תבוב תבקן את הבאר בגביר
(יש תרסיו!) ואבא תבב תע בבל של
ואבא בא יעפס ברבב את האבל בבלם
או הבחו נתן בן ואבו בה חובה, עם ואת
ואבא עברת מתבר עבד וארבות : "ארבה יא סבר".
ואבבא הבתה בארבר תעב
מתחה עבבר, ואבא רה הבאן אבא כבר
(ואבא שמתחשך על עבבו את הבאן) לבבת בבין
(נכסת פאן!!) האבון

אבא לא רות
הכל
אתם
הורים נפלאים!!

להרור שרתחבה ש מתחים מאבם רק
ושמצרים צב בבה באבא אלהבים
עבשיו אנחנו באבא ויצים פתא
הורים מבג בומוי

מאותנו: אלברי, יצבה, ונתמחו

Dear Abba and Ima

We're so glad you came home,
Back to our routine — both the good and bad.
Again, there will be the wonderful smells of cooking,
Again, Abba will play practical jokes.
Again, Ima will call us to come and eat,
And Abba won't stop wolfing down the food.
Abba will grumble,
"Why didn't you mop up the bathroom?
Someone could slip!"
Ima will say, "You don't need to turn on the lights.
You can open the shutters,"
And..."Please feed Buffy."

When Abba comes home, this is what happens:
Everyone kisses him on the cheek.
Ima goes from room to room, complaining
"What a mess!"
Most of the time Ima works in the garden.
If Abba feels like it, he turns on the lawnmower.

But in spite of everything, you're great parents!
Sometimes there's tension, of course,
But when you're far away.
We realize how much we love you.
And when you get back we're all happy,
Because now we know you're awesome parents.

From us —
Ofri, Ye'ela and Bat-Chen

To Our Mother

Mother's Day is the one time in the year
When we say thank you for all the years.
We stop and look around us, and realize
That we all owe you so much.
Quarrels and arguments can't be prevented,
And eventually good things result from anger and tension.
It's true that sometimes you're angry, but the sages said,
"A mother who doesn't get angry isn't a good one."
Though it could sound strange,
This sentence is trying to express
That a mother who doesn't slap,
Who doesn't shout when things get out of hand,
Who doesn't guide and explain,
Is a mother who doesn't care about her kids,
Who isn't worried if her children don't study
And grow into good people.

We're the car and you're the steering wheel.
If we're not driven properly there could be an accident.
It's the steering wheel that says when to turn left or right.
And when we're approaching an intersection,
It must choose the best direction for a safe journey.

Ima, you have taught us so many things.
You always tell us to show respect for others —
That we don't live in a vacuum.
You have said that all of us are equal,
There are no differences among us.
You have told us that everything God created
Has a tiny flaw.
You have told us that every human being has virtues,
Even though we don't always want to see them.
You have told us that in life you must look for friends.
Because enemies are waiting everywhere.

A few words to sum up:
Though it may seem
That sometimes our relationship is one of anger and hate,
There's so much concern and love inside it.
And so we've brought you lovely flowers,
Ima, I don't know about other mothers,
But we really mean it, these aren't just words.

To our beautiful, smart Ima who helps and understands,
whose chief trait is her integrity, who fights for the rights
of her children, the best Ima in the world. Remember we
will love you forever!

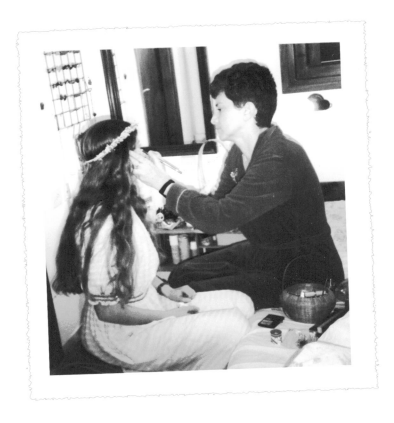

To Dad

Behind every animal is hidden a characteristic of someone in my family. So let's begin:

The butterfly — Ye'ela:
She loves to be free
And do as she pleases.
To have her head in the clouds,
And to have a great time.

The dove — Ima
Always calming our arguments
    and storms.
She wants us live in peace
    and quiet,
Like a family should.
She always says:
"It's so easy to make enemies,
But it's wiser to find friends."

The worm — Ofri:
He looks so innocent,
But it's not so at all.
He's a real smart aleck.
He can cause a uproar.
But when he wants to,
He can be wonderful.

The tortoise — Abba:
Who carries everything
    on his back.
He has a double responsibility:
To his work and to his family.

The cat — Bat-Chen:
Actually cats and I
Are really very different:
Cats are clean and neat.
And I'm surrounded by mess.
Cats prefer to walk alone,
And I'm always on the phone.
So remember me as a special girl,
Who's a little different.

To Ofri

Ofri's a great kid. When you ask him,
"How are you?" and "How was it?"
He always says, "Great!"
He loves to work in the garden,
And he also loves Noam.
He loves bulldozers and Abba's tools.
He loves Buffy the dog, and baking cakes with Ima.
He can even swallow his pills, and loves that too.
But he hates wearing sandals.

I'm writing you three months late.
I know it's not right that you're getting this seder night.
But you know what they say: "Better late than never!"

You're such a special aunt; there's no one else like you.
We can have fun and do silly things together.
We can talk about interesting things,
Not just about how big the kids have grown,
And how to cook things.
You can't keep still, and are running
From here to there...and back again.
You're a busy woman but you always find time for family.
You have green eyes and a gorgeous figure.
You know when to be silly and when to be serious.
Your warmth and zest for life surround you with friends.

Noam, you're a beautiful, stunning young woman
Who always says that you have to have fun...
Because we live only once.
You always get what you want,
And you know that good investments pay off.
When people meet you they can't hide their smiles.
You're on our same wavelength and that's really cool.

So Mazal Tov, despite being late.
I hope this card was worth the wait.
We're sending you all the good wishes in the world.
We'll love you forever and never forget you.

May you reach 120.
Or when you reach 100, may you feel like 20.

To Hadas

(13th birthday greeting sent to Hadas Dror, on left in photo, who was killed together with Bat-Chen in the Dizengoff bombing)

Each year, you climb another step,
Each year you change a little.
And every time you go up higher,
It's as if you're telling everyone:
"Look, I'm growing up; soon I'll be an adult!"
Wait a bit, young woman, it doesn't happen so fast.
People don't grow up that quickly.
Come, let's think back and try to remember.

From zero to one you were the light of your family.
Because of you, two young people had become parents.
But you taught your brand new parents
How to care for kids.

From one to two you discovered that you had legs.
You started walking and falling,
And didn't give up until you stood on them firmly.

From two to three you started to talk.
First you mumbled words,
And then you made them into sentences.

From three to four you spoke clearly,
And walked confidently.
You played with dolls and made friends in nursery school.

From four to five you gave up your pacifier,
Together with the bottle that you hadn't used in a while.
They were packed away in boxes. No need for them now.

From six to seven you started first grade.
You were somewhat fearful.
It was new and unknown: the children and teachers.
Suddenly, you were bombarded with words.
But in the end it all worked out.

And so the years raced by,
From first grade to second to third and so on.
Every year as you faced new challenges,
You learned from your mistakes.
You built on your experience, trying to get it right.

There were many problems and obstacles.
But with them, there were happy and cheerful things too.
They say: There's no good without bad, and that's life.

Now that you're grown you're expected to help,
Looking after your brothers, doing housework, etc.
It's not easy to be grown-up, but it can be fun,
Especially now that boys are starting to come around.

OK, enough philosophy and nice words.
I wanted to dedicate these lines to you:
Hadas, you're a terrific friend.
You're willing to give encouragement when needed.
You know how to accept all differences,
And to help those who are weak.
You're a beautiful, smart girl.
And you deserve lots of admiration!

May your life be happy.
And may you live among people who love you.

Mazal Tov!

To Ima

On this day, 39 years ago. you entered the world
And started life like everyone else.
And because of that day, we're all here now.
Dear Ima, we don't always know how to thank you,
And we don't always know how to ask forgiveness.
So we want to take this opportunity,
Because we think it's the place and time, and particularly the day,
To tell you that you're a wonderful mother.

Sometimes we get angry, of course,
And it looks as if we hate you,
But afterwards when we calm down,
We understand that you were right,
And you just want the best for us children.
You're always concerned, always protecting us from danger.
You always say that we learn from mistakes,
And if you never try, you never know.
All through the years you've given us education and values,
Teaching us how to behave like good people.
You introduced us into the world, explained and advised.
And in times of trouble you always have good suggestions
And help us figure out how to solve a problem.

We'll always remember your famous saying,
That reflects your character and life experiences:
"It's easy to make enemies, but it's wiser to find friends."
What else should we say that hasn't already been said?
Until we were born, your life was easier.
And then we were born, and things got harder.
We screamed, and you had to change our diapers.
And even after we grew up, the problems didn't end.
We fought and quarreled, and studied now and then.
Still one thing is very clear – we all love you.

To Our Abba

He's tall, with a round potbelly.
Maybe that's why his heart is so big,
With room for everyone.
His blue eyes have a sparkle of mischief.
Sometimes he's a child trapped in a grown-up's body.
And we're sure though time has passed,
He's remained a child.

Food is one of Abba's hobbies,
Particularly anything sweet.
He's always looking for candy,
And Ima always finds new places to hide it.
When he finds the candy, it vanishes at once,
Swallowed up in his big tummy.

When we were little, we waited for the evening.
You would tell us stories about *Tarzan, King of the Apes,*
And *Snow White and the Seven Dwarfs.*
The stories always ended with the heroes
Living in wealth and happiness for the rest of their lives.

Now that we've grown up, the roles have changed.
Instead we tell you stories
About school, friends, and teachers,
And you listen and solve our problems.
Afterward, life seems much better.

Becoming parents isn't like getting a driver's licence,
Where you pass a test and get a certificate.
It's like taking a kid of four who's never swum before
And throwing him into a pool.
At first he swims awkwardly,
But slowly he learns
And in the end he manages to swim.

Dad, this is a bit late,
But we really hope it was worth waiting for.
You probably say: It's a good thing I have a birthday.
At least once a year they remember to say a few words.
But it's not like that at all.
We think about you every day,
Though sometimes you give us a hard time!
When it's nine o'clock with no sign of life from you,
The whole family gets nervous.
We worry and try to think of other things,
But we just can't.
You're deep inside each of us.
Each has his own special Abba
And can't live without him.

To Dear Yoav, Itai, Hila and Ro'ee

Like a fading flower that suddenly blooms again,
The New Year begins, ends, and starts anew.
With every beginning there is anticipation.
We put the past behind
And gallop towards the future.

We want to send you our wishes:
May you always hear birdsong, never thunder,
May you always see flowers in bloom,
Never a field of thistles.
It all depends on how we look at things.
And whether we start the new year full of despair
Or full of hope.

So may the new year fulfill all of your wishes.
May it be the best year ever,
Successful and productive.
May you get everything you want.
May the good win out over the bad,
And sadness lose out to joy.
Together with all this, we send you lots of kisses.

Make good use of the year in the best way possible,
Because we only live once.
So have yourselves a glorious time.

Now can you guess what we're waiting for?
We're waiting for next year,
When you'll all be visiting our little country.
That will really be a wonderful New Year!

To Ye'ela

When God created us He mixed good and bad,
But with you He got a little bit confused,
And all the bad rolled away.

You turned out a beautiful child
With blue eyes and blond hair.
A girl with a golden heart who is considerate of others,
And is always ready to help.
But you have a talent for being dramatic,
So sometimes people don't actually know
Whether it's for real or one of your games.

Such an energetic, active girl who can't sit still,
And has to be on the move the whole day through.
You're great at sports — basketball, high-jump, running,
And you've got proof, because you fall an awful lot.
You love having fun, but hate hiking.
Just give you water slides and you're ecstatic,
Though the word "museum" isn't in your vocabulary.

Our relationship can get rocky.
Sometimes we're really close and sometimes so far apart,
But you're always important to me.
I hope you know my door is always open.

May you always make good decisions,
Know how to compromise, and where to draw the line —
Between what's allowed and what's forbidden.
Now you've joined the grown-up world,
Which is very demanding.
But I'm sure you can succeed.

Lots of love and all the good wishes in the world. I'll
always love you and never forget you. And everything I've
written here came straight from my heart.

To Nili On Her Bat Mitzvah

Whenever I write greetings I try to be totally original, and
not repeat all the trite stuff about "living until 120."
Something special is needed, because a greeting should fit
the person. It should not be just another boring
composition. The big question is what does that person
really want to be?

Some people want to be rich and count their pennies,
one by one, day by day. Someone else would be happiest
living alone on a mountain. There are girls who want to
be (no more, no less) fashion models. Another might
dream of being the girl all the boys are crazy about, the
girl who breaks hearts. "I'm in a daze. She's so
beautiful."

Some people hope to become famous, the person
everyone talks about. Others simply want to be happy,
singing all day long. Essentially everyone wants to be
happy, though each person takes a different path to
achieve it. Because all roads lead to happiness.

So, Nilush! Take whichever road you want, but
remember that the main thing is to be happy. I hope
you'll be able to fulfill all your dreams for the future,
and that you always stay my Nili – with all your pluses
and minuses. And may that lucky man come along
who steals your heart and teaches you what love is
and how delicious it can be if you just treat it properly—
like life itself.

But wherever you go, don't ever forget that you've got a
place in my heart, that you're a special girl, and most

important, I love you terribly. Your talent for writing and drawing are like those of the very best poets and artists, and I won't exaggerate if I say that some of them are overshadowed by you. Do me a favor: continue to blossom into a beautiful young woman on the outside, but inside, there's no need to change.

Love you very, very, very much

Note : Nili survived the terrorist attack at Dizengoff

*T*o Grandma On Her 60th Birthday

It's easy to see why we love you.
You radiate so much love and affection.
On birthdays people are always full of praise.
But we're not just saying nice words.
This is simply what we feel,
You'd be the first to say there's no arguing with feelings.

You show we're important to you in so many ways.
You prepare tasty dishes, take us to museums,
Buy us things, and come to visit.
Maybe we don't always show how much we love you.
So this may be the place and time to tell you
That we'll never forget you.

In tough situations, when everything seems to collapse,
You always know how to encourage us.
You entertain us and our tears dry right away.
You say the right words at the right time.
And if you have to scold us, you do it just right.
Grandma, you teach us about life.
You've explained there are all sorts of people
And there's no choice - we have to get along with them.
You tell us to watch how we behave,
And why it's worth making others happy.
Because you've experienced life,
You explain how to get out of tough situations,
Even though you're 60,
Your spirit and nature are more like a 20-year-old.

Your one clear goal is for us to grow into good people,
And we promise eventually
We'll put your advice into practice.

At the moment it's all theoretical, we're still learning.
But in future we'll apply everything you've said.

Even the most brilliant poet
Can't describe your character,
Compared to you, words and letters seem small
And sometimes there just aren't enough words.

So, Happy Birthday. May you live until 120.
Please don't ever change, and always be our grandmother,
So loving and understanding and special.
May you always know, till the end of days,
That we're proud of you.
And if now and then we're angry, we're always loving.

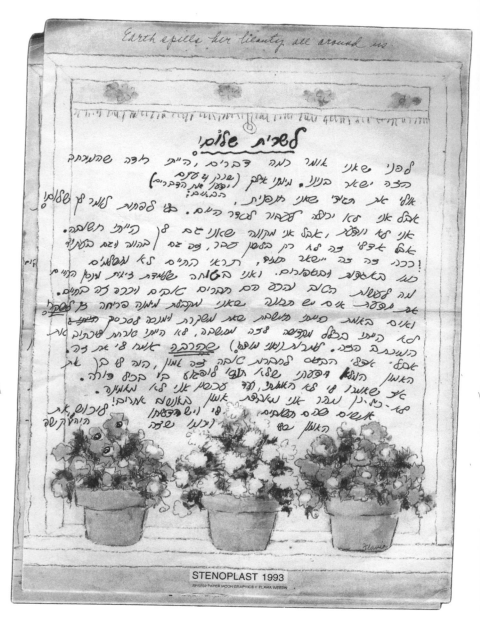

Original Hebrew of letter to Sarit on page 92.

Letters
& Eulogies

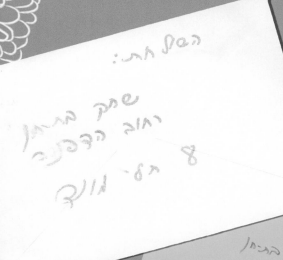

*D*ear Sarit *(an unsent letter)*

Before I start, I want this letter to remain between us —
only four eyes should see what follows. You may think
I'm flattering you, but I just can't get back to my normal
routine without at least saying goodbye.

I hope that I was also important to you. For me, though,
it's not only in the past tense, it's in the present and
future. Look, life isn't perfect like in fairytales, and I
expect you've learned that from experience. Good and
bad are always friends. If there's one quality that gives
me a rash, it's lying! And if I really thought you were
lying, I wouldn't even take the time to write this letter.

But that's what people have told me. For me the basis of
friendship is trust. I really trusted you so I didn't believe
them, and I still don't believe them. I don't lose trust so
quickly.

I don't know if this will turn out to be a farewell letter.
Perhaps my pink pen will change the decision. But the
ball is now in your court. Just remember that I loved you
and always will. And when I think back (like an old
woman remembering her childhood) I see how great we
were together, what fun we had, the way we giggled in
class and hid our notes from the teachers. We were so
busy matchmaking, the last thing that interested us were
classes. The gorgeous guys were more interesting!

So before you make a decision, just give it some thought.
I don't change girlfriends every few days as if they were a
pair of socks. You said yourself that if I make up with
Leehee, we could go on being friends! What she did was
really nasty, but she apologized and she can't do more
than that. Everyone makes mistakes. But our friendship

93

shouldn't suffer because of this! She cried for us to make up, and I have a conscience. What would you have done in my place? I really didn't think it meant losing you! Okay, I've said what I wanted to say.

P.S. If you decide to make up, please call me.

*S*ometimes

Sometimes you get lost and need encouragement.
Sometime life seems black,
As if God didn't make any other colors.
Sometimes you seem to be in a minefield
With no way out.
Sometimes you want to escape all your problems,
And remain somewhere in a dream world.

Sometime you just can't understand why flowers bloom.
Sometimes you think there's no hope left,
No light at the end of the tunnel.

Sometimes you want the waves to wash you away
And never bring you back.
Sometimes you want to break down the barriers,
And sometimes all your illusions shatter.
Sometimes others don't seem to understand

Because they're not in the same situation.
They have no idea what they're saying.

Sometimes life is like the sea;
Calm one day and stormy the next.
And the day after the storm we walk on smooth sand.

Sometimes we love, sometimes we hate,
And then we discover that these two emotions,
Which are said to be opposites, are actually very close.

Sometimes we're sad with no reason.
It's hard to explain.
It's like a virus that comes and goes.

Sometimes they don't seem to love you,
They don't pay attention,
They're not the people you know.
Suddenly they're strangers.

And sometimes you think you're alone.
Everyone's left you.
Sometimes you think: Why?
Is there something the matter with me?
Why do they hurt me? Are they all so perfect?

And sometimes, sometimes, things happen to us.
But you have to remember that it's only sometimes.

Leehee, I love you and always will.

To Grandpa!

We face the grave, and another tear falls.
A cold grave looks back at us.
Oh, it's just not you!
The words are so harsh and threatening,
Nothing like you at all.
But we have to respect them.
Because it's the last memory.
This is your house and we're the guests.
So we'll be polite.

The tears keep falling, loving and concerned.
They want to penetrate the cold stone.
If only they could warm your body a little.
They just can't believe.
"It makes no sense."
Only yesterday he hugged me,
Only yesterday he stood here at my side.
They promise to remember you.
And to keep you in our hearts.

ירושלים

Jerusalem

My Jerusalem

Even before I could walk, I was in Jerusalem.
My grandmother lives there,
And on each visit we would wander —
To the museums, Meah Shearim,
Liberty Bell Park and the Karon Theater,
To the Kotel, the Flour Mill, and other places.

And each time, I'm newly amazed
At the stunning beauty of Jerusalem,
And all of its wonderful places.
That's why I've decided to take you
On a trip around Jerusalem,
So you can see its magnificent scenery for yourself,
And meet its special people,
And form your own opinion of Jerusalem.

The Arabs in Jerusalem

When people say
That everyone lives together in Jerusalem,
It's more than just words.
And that's the beauty of it.
Because, just beside the Western Wall,
Is a Muslim mosque.
Jerusalem is also sacred to the Arabs,
And they also have many interesting sites —
The mosques, the market, and the bakeries -
The places that represent them.

Arabs and Jews live alongside each other.
So, in some way, Jerusalem is a symbol of peace,
Evidence that it's possible for us to live together
And enjoy the sacred splendor of Jerusalem.

Jerusalem by Night

One of the loveliest sights is the sunset.
It's an awesome spectacle.
And particularly in Jerusalem it is something magnificent.
The beautiful tones of the gold and red walls
Blend and create an enchanting view.

Religious People in Jerusalem

Beautiful poems have been written about you
By people in awe of your stunning beauty.
In this one city, it's possible to find so many things.
But wherever you look,
There are religious people in front of you.
Dressed in long, black, belted suits. It must be so hot!

It was Friday and everybody was getting ready:
Going to the central market,
Buying everything they need:
Meat, challah, candles, and kippot.
The names of the shops come from the Bible.
Posters, too, are written in the language of old texts.
It's so old-fashioned.

We went into some shops.
Typically, they sold candles and kippot and Bibles.
Religious Jews live and breathe the Torah,
It is the center of their lives.
Day and night they pray.
Upholding values and beliefs different from ours.

But it was nice to see how, under your nose in tiny Israel,
Religious people seem to have built their own country,
Closed and cut off from their surroundings.

The Kotel (Western Wall)

The Wall is lichen and lead,
Some people have hearts of stone,
Some stones have a human heart.

When problems crop up,
Many of us face the Kotel and pour out our tears,
Hoping that the day comes when everything will be OK.
Pushing a note between the cracks of the huge stones,
Which sometimes — like in the words above —
Understand more than human beings do.
Though they never speak and never answer.

These stones have gone through so much.
People came and kissed them in the War of Independence.
Jerusalem was captured, and after it was freed
So many thrilling stories were told.

It's a holy place for Jews.
This is where they pray on the holidays,
And regular days too.
Only the Western Wall is left.

When I visited it I was very scared,
And looked over my shoulder all the time,
To see that there were no Arabs.
And that's why I wrote in my note:
"May there be peace, so we can walk safely
Through the streets of the Old City."

Peace

In 8th grade, because of her commitment to peace and co-existence, Bat-Chen chose to participate in a pen-pal project. She exchanged letters with Nidaa, a young Arab girl who lives in Kfar Kassim near Petach Tikvah. This is a letter from Nidaa.

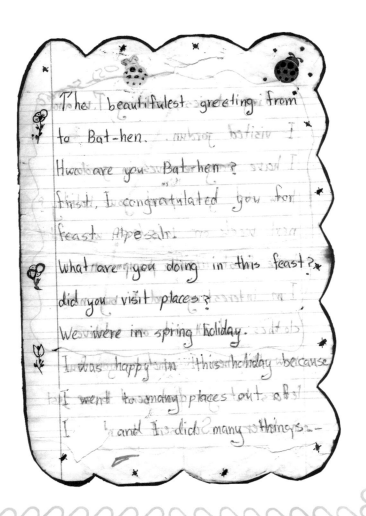

The beautifulest greeting from
to Bat-hen.
Huw are you Bat-hen?
first, I congratulated you for
feast Alpesah.
What are you doing in this feast?
did you visit places?
We were in spring holiday.
I was happy in this holiday because
I went to many places out of
I and the did many things

reading stories, watching T.v and

I visited jordun.

I have many relatives in jurolon.

how did you spend your holiday?

next week on 10/5/95 we will

have fest Aladha جماعة on

I'm interesting and I buy new

clothes and I'll visit our relative

now But then I send to you four

letters but you don't send to me just

on letter. So sent to m

Bat-Chen began to write in English, but found it difficult and asked her friend Leehee for help. This is a text that she gave Leehee to translate.

Leehee: Please write the following things to Nidaa:

My hobbies are reading, writing, watching TV, and horseback riding. I was happy to receive her letter and I am sorry that I am sending mine so late. I look forward to meeting her. My birthday is March 19. I support the peace process. I hate math. I live in Tel Mond.

Please bring the letter to me as soon as you can!

Hello Nida, I

Dear Bat-hen

How are you?

I am fine.

I hope you will have
happy "new" year.

"good - by"

Marble Forum, Salamis, Cyprus
Salamis was founded by Teucer, a hero of the Trojan War and
the son of King Telamon of Salamis (Greece) in the 12th
century B.C. Salamis was the leading city of Cyprus for
a thousand years and it was the biggest commercial centre
of the Eastern Mediterranean. In the 4th century A. D. the
city was destroyed by earthquakes and rebuilt by the Emperor
Constantine who named it Constantia. The city was attacked
in different periods by Persians, Romans, Egyptians and, finally,
was destroyed by the Arabs in 648.
DT-4572-D © DCC Ltd., 1974

Post Card

from "Nidaa" to
"Bathen"

Poem To Peace

Peace is a kind of dream
That holds only good things —
An easy life with no complications.
Because when there is peace,
There are no enemies,
And you're not horrified, over and over again,
At the sight of another terrorist attack.

War and Peace

War is a terrible thing. It takes away the most beautiful
gift we've been given – life. Because of it, bereaved
mothers stand facing the grave in disbelief. And in their
innermost heart, they hope that it didn't really happen,
that it's simply a bad dream.

A Summary of War and Peace

There is not much left to say.
We're in a sort of in a middle ground.
There isn't real peace in the Middle East,
Nor is there real war.

And we are marching forward towards peace,
Ready to understand the other side,
Prepared to make changes,
With one clear goal:
To be rid of the hatred
Buried deep inside us for so long.
And with the understanding
That it's easy to make enemies.
But the wise thing is to find friends.

We come as people who know a lot about war,
But very little about peace.
From now on we'll begin to change that.

These words cover years and years
Of suffering, pain, anxiety and fear.
Now to all these words we add a new word: hope.
A little strange, a little different perhaps.
In fact it was with us all along (even in war).
And because of it,
We never remained alone in the struggle.

Yet, if we talk about peace, we cannot conclude
Without the song that became the hymn of peace.
The hope that remains with us all our lives:

"He who extinguishes his candle is buried in ashes."

Golan Anxiety

Crowds of settlers from the Golan Heights demonstrated today, holding up signs reading, "Rabin has no mandate over the Golan," "The Land of Israel is in danger," and "We must not withdraw." The dozens of settlers, many of whom wore knitted kippot, scorned the government, demanded that Prime Minister Rabin be dismissed, and proposed a vote of no-confidence in the government. Many of the settlers came to demonstrate today, so that they would not be forced to leave their homes and work, and change their way of life.

With all due respect to the settlers, for whom the Land of Israel (in particular "Greater Israel") is so important, I just don't understand. If the country is so important to them, why do they refuse to give up the Golan, so we can live in peace in a safer country. It's all political: the Right is against it, and the Left is for it. If we do nothing and just mark time, it won't help. We must move ahead, step by step. Otherwise there will never be peace, and it will remain nothing more than a dream.

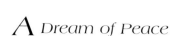

A Dream of Peace

Every person has a dream.
One wants to be a millionaire,
Another wants to be a writer,
And I have a dream
About peace.

Sometimes we despair,
And feel that the special day —
When every one will be happy and united,
Right and left,
Arabs and Jews,
Become partners and friends,
And there is no hatred and war anymore —
That unique day looks like it won't come.

Maybe I'm just a naïve girl, who doesn't
    know anything,
But is it too much to ask for peace
    and security?
Is it too much to dream
Of walking securely in the streets of the
    Old City?
Is it too much to ask that we not have
    to watch
Mothers of young soldiers crying on their graves?

Afterword

I would have loved so much to thank Bat-Chen in person for her striking, caring words. But I shall never have that chance. Bat-Chen was killed in the terrorist bombing at Dizengoff Center in March 1996, along with two of her girlfriends. Several weeks after the bombing, I visited the families of these three 15-year-old girls. Even after the devastating loss of his daughter, Bat-Chen's father had the courage to say to me personally, and publicly on Israeli television, that he supported the peace process as passionately as his daughter had.

Leah Rabin

Leah Rabin, second from right, with Bat-Chen's parents
-- father Tzvika on the left and mother Ayelet on the right --
at the dedication of Yitzhak Rabin High School in Tel Mond.

In Memoriam

Yuval Levy - Age 13

Koby Zaharon - Age 13

Hadas Dror - Age 15

Dana Gutterman - Age 15

Bat-Chen Shahak - Age 15

Assaf Wax - Age 22

Inbar Attiya - Age 23

Tali Gordon - Age 25

Gail Belkin - Age 48

Danny Tversky - Age 58

Leah Misrahi - Age 63

Silvia Bernstain - Age 75

Rachel Sela - Age 82